TROY PERCIVAL

CHUCK FINLEY

BOB BOONE

DEAN CHANCE

BOBBY GRICH

DOUG DeCINCES

DARIN ERSTAD

ROD CAREW

WALLY JOYNER

NOLAN RYAN

TROY GLAUS

REGGIE JACKSON

THE HISTORY OF THE
ANAHEIM
ANGELS

WAYNE STEWART

CREATIVE ᏟᏆ EDUCATION

Published by Creative Education, 123 South Broad Street, Mankato, MN 56001.

Creative Education is an imprint of The Creative Company.

Designed by Rita Marshall.

Photographs by AllSport (Stephen Dunn, Jeff Gross, Jed Jacobsohn), Associated Press/Wide World

Photos, Icon Sports Media (John Cordes), Anthony Neste, Sports Gallery (Al Messerschmidt),

SportsChrome (Rob Tringali Jr., Michael Zito)

Library of Congress Cataloging-in-Publication Data

Stewart, Wayne, 1951- The history of the Anaheim Angels / by Wayne Stewart.

p. cm. — (Baseball)   ISBN 1-58341-198-4

Summary: A team history of the baseball franchise that played in Los Angeles

until their move to Anaheim, California, in 1966.

1. Anaheim Angels (Baseball team)—History—

Juvenile literature. [1. Anaheim Angels (Baseball team)—History.

2. Baseball—History.] I. Title. II. Baseball (Mankato, Minn.).

GV875.A58 S84 2002   796.357'64'0979496—dc21   2001047856

First Edition 9 8 7 6 5 4 3 2 1

WHEN THE CITY

was surrounded by orange groves. Today, this Los Angeles suburb is

best known as the home of Disneyland and other popular tourist

attractions. One favorite attraction for visitors and locals alike is

Edison Field, home of the city's professional baseball team, the

Anaheim Angels.

The Angels came into existence in 1960, when the American

League (AL) decided to create teams in Los Angeles and

Washington, D.C., expanding the league to 10 teams. The AL

awarded a team to wealthy movie star Gene Autry, and his team

began play in 1961 as the Los Angeles Angels. The team has changed

its name and location since those days, but the Angels have always

LEON WAGNER

enjoyed the steady support of West Coast fans.

{EARLY ANGELS STARS} The 1961 Angels finished the season

in eighth place, but their win-loss percentage (.435)

was higher than any expansion team in history.

The following season, they improved by 16 victories,

shooting up to third place in the AL with an 86–76

record. In fact, they ended up only 10 games behind

the first-place powerhouse New York Yankees.

A year after losing 18 games in one road trip, the **1962** Angels won 14 games in one road trip.

6

Helping to fuel this great start was hard-hitting outfielder

Leon Wagner, who drilled 28, 37, and 26 home runs from 1961 to

1963. Another Angels star during those early years was pitcher

Dean Chance. In 1964, Chance was downright dominant, posting a

microscopic 1.65 ERA. "You ever hear of a year like I had?" he

boasted. "I led the league in wins, with 20. I had the lowest ERA in

both leagues."

GARRET ANDERSON

In **1964**, Dean Chance became the Angels' first (and only) Cy Young Award winner.

DEAN CHANCE

Jim Fregosi, an intense shortstop known for his superb defensive play, also helped to lead the Angels' charge. Fregosi was a solid but unspectacular hitter. Yet somehow he always seemed to get on base and was a steady run producer throughout his career. Always an intelligent player and valuable leader, he went on to become a big-league manager (including a stint with the Angels) after his playing days were over.

One of the first Angels greats, Jim Fregosi played in six All-Star Games during the **1960s** and '**70s**.

The Angels remained a formidable team throughout the mid-1960s. In 1965, the team was renamed the California Angels and moved from Los Angeles to nearby Anaheim. In the years that followed, the Angels improved considerably by adding two talented pitchers: right-hander Andy Messersmith and lefty Clyde Wright. Of the two, Wright made the quickest impact, cementing his status as one of the league's top hurlers by winning 22 games in 1970.

JIM FREGOSI

Despite a history full of terrific players, Anaheim is still seeking its first world title.

DAVID ECKSTEIN

With his outgoing personality and thick Southern accent, he also became an Angels fan favorite.

The **1975** Angels were one of the quickest teams in the league, stealing a club-record 220 bases.

The 1970 season was also the campaign in which Alex Johnson became the only Angels player ever to win a batting crown. The sometimes surly outfielder, who was often at odds with the media but appreciated by teammates, hit .329 to lead all AL batters.

Johnson's great season at the plate helped the Angels tie their franchise high for wins, going 86–76.

{THE RYAN EXPRESS} From 1972 to 1979, the Angels were led by one of the greatest pitchers in baseball history: Nolan Ryan. Although seven of those eight seasons were losing ones for California, the young flamethrower kept fans riveted. In July 1973, Ryan struck out 17 batters while throwing his second no-hitter of the season. In all, he amassed a staggering seven career no-hitters—

NOLAN RYAN

four of them while wearing an Angels uniform—and played a

major-league record 27 seasons.

Ryan's wicked fastball often topped 100 miles per hour.

Amazingly, his pitches were still clocked in the mid-90s during his

final season at the age of 46. "When you talk velocity, Nolan threw

the hardest," said Angels catcher Jeff Torborg. "Nolan threw it down the strike zone harder than any human being I ever saw. In 1973, against the Boston Red Sox, Nolan threw a pitch a little up and over my left shoulder. I reached up for it and Nolan's pitch tore a hole in the webbing of my glove and hit the backstop at Fenway Park."

In 1979, Ryan's final season with California, the Angels won the AL Western Division (the league was

14 divided into two divisions in 1969). Frank Tanana, a brilliant left-handed pitcher, teamed with Ryan to give the Angels one of the league's most feared one-two punches that season. One sportswriter described their effect on opposing hitters as "Tanana and Ryan and a lot of cryin'."

Rugged outfielder Don Baylor led California's offense in 1979 by slamming 36 home runs and driving in 139 RBI—efforts that earned him the AL Most Valuable Player (MVP) award. Three other

> In **1979**, three Angels players drove in at least 100 runs (Don Baylor, Bobby Grich, and Dan Ford).

DARIN ERSTAD

key players that season were utility man Brian Downing, second

baseman Bobby Grich, and first baseman Rod Carew. Downing was

a fan favorite in California for 14 seasons, and Grich was one of the

game's best defensive second basemen.

Carew, meanwhile, combined a great eye and amazing bat

control to become perhaps the game's best hitter. "He handled the bat with the same efficiency Merlin coaxed from his wand," noted a

writer for *The Sporting News.* "Rod Carew was a baseball magician

with the power to make well-placed pitches

disappear into every conceivable outfield gap."

Carew was a superb two-strike hitter. Using a

light bat, he would wait on the ball until the last

instant. Then, he'd flick the bat and swat line drives

Rod Carew
became the
16th player in
major-league
history to
collect 3,000
hits in his
career.

to all parts of the field. He won seven batting crowns during his first

12 seasons in the majors and antagonized AL pitchers for 19 seasons.

"He could bunt .300 if he tried," New York Yankees manager Billy

Martin once said.

{TWO MORE TITLES} The Angels lost to the Baltimore Orioles

in the 1979 AL Championship Series (ALCS), but they rebounded

quickly. In 1982, California set a franchise record with a 93–69 mark

and won its division. Sadly, the team was then derailed in the ALCS

ROD CAREW

The Angels
have been
waging battle
on the West
Coast for more
than four
decades.

again, losing the final three games of the best-of-five series to the

Milwaukee Brewers.

Reggie Jackson was an all-or-nothing hitter in **1982**, leading the AL in home runs and strikeouts.

Still, Angels fans took consolation in the promise of their star-studded lineup. In addition to Grich, Baylor, Carew, and swift center fielder Fred Lynn, California featured future Hall-of-Famer Reggie Jackson, a powerful outfielder. Jackson, who went on to clout

20 more than 500 home runs in his career, bopped an AL-best 39 homers in 1982. Such offensive firepower made up for his notoriously porous defense. "It's not that Reggie is a bad outfielder," big-league manager Billy Martin joked. "He just has trouble judging the ball and picking it up."

In 1986, the Angels clawed their way to a 92–70 record and won the AL West once again. The ace of the Angels' pitching staff that season was 6-foot-7 Mike Witt, who mowed down opposing

REGGIE JACKSON

hitters en route to a career-high 18 victories. Witt led the Angels

into the playoffs, where they met the Boston Red Sox in the ALCS.

The series was a fierce struggle that went a full seven games, but in

the end, the Angels fell again.

Although the 1986 playoffs were another letdown, Angels fans

continued to enjoy the performances of a number of talented

players. Star catcher Bob Boone remained a steadying influence on the team throughout the mid-1980s. The durable backstop caught more games than any player other than Hall-of-Famer Carlton Fisk and won seven Gold Glove awards for his brilliant defense.

Doug DeCinces, another standout of the mid-1980s, may well have been the team's best third

22 baseman ever. DeCinces was instrumental in California's division-winning seasons in 1982 and 1986, coming up with two of his best hitting seasons those years (swatting 30 and 26 home runs, respectively). Angels fans also enjoyed watching the heroics of center fielder Devon White, whose long stride and great acceleration made him a marvelous base stealer and defender.

{A PROLONGED SLUMP} From 1987 to 1994, California suffered some lean years. In 1989, the Angels compiled a solid 91–71

BOB BOONE

Star Doug DeCinces averaged 22 home runs a season during his six-year Angels career.

DOUG DeCINCES

record but finished in third place in their division. Other than that, it was a string of mostly mediocre seasons for the Angels.

Still, California continued to produce some splendid players. Among them was ace pitcher Chuck Finley, a lefty who led the Angels in the late 1980s and most of the '90s. Finley stood 6-foot-7 and instilled fear in opposing batters with his wicked splitter and equally nasty fastball. No Angels pitcher ever won more games (165) than Finley. And what Finley started, reliever Bryan Harvey often finished. Harvey rang up save after save during those years, including an AL-leading 46 in 1991.

Another Angels standout of the late 1980s and early '90s was first baseman Wally Joyner. In 1986, Joyner became the first rookie ever elected to the starting lineup of the All-Star Game, and he only got better in the seasons that followed. The always-popular Joyner

CHUCK FINLEY

hit as many as 34 homers (1987) and was a steady run producer

year after year. "He's a spray hitter who's very adept at going with a

pitch. . . . He's especially hard to fan. . . . Joyner loves to hit in the

clutch," read one big-league scout's assessment.

Angels fans also enjoyed watching pitcher Mark Langston and

outfielder Chili Davis in the early '90s. The lanky Langston won

Gold Glove awards in five consecutive seasons and frustrated

opponents with his blazing fastball. Davis, meanwhile, played for

the Angels for eight seasons and earned a reputation as

one of the most prolific power-hitting switch-hitters in

baseball history, battering the ball to all fields.

{STARS OF THE '90s} In 1995, the Angels

went 78–67 and finished in second place in their

division—their best showing in nine years. They then posted winning

In **1990**, Mark Langston and Mike Witt combined to pitch the eighth no-hitter in club history.

records again in 1997 and 1998. One reason for the improvement

was the play of outfielder Jim Edmonds. In 1997, the first

season the team was known as the Anaheim Angels, Edmonds

earned a Gold Glove award for his sure mitt in the outfield.

Edmonds was just one of several talented outfielders on

the Angels' roster in the late 1990s. The team also featured

Garret Anderson, who posted a team-record 28-game hitting streak

MARK LANGSTON

27

in 1998, and Darin Erstad, a former college football star and superb

defensive player. Yet another member of Anaheim's great outfield

Fearful of his
mighty swing,
pitchers
walked Tim
Salmon 95
times during
the **1997**
season.
was Tim Salmon, a tremendous fastball hitter. In 1997,

Salmon crushed 33 homers and racked up 129 RBI.

"Tim's one of those guys who, when they hit the ball, it

makes a different sound," said Angels shortstop Gary

DiSarcina. "For most guys, you hear the regular crack.

28 When Tim hits one, it's like thunder. BOOM!"

Also crushing the ball during those years was third baseman

Troy Glaus. Born in Tarzana, California, the 6-foot-5 and 245-pound

slugger possessed Tarzan-like strength. In 2000, at the age of 24,

Glaus won his first AL home run crown by swatting 47 round-

trippers. "Troy Glaus has learned how to hit the ball the other way,

and he has power to all fields," noted one big-league scout. "We

might be looking at a home run champion for years to come. He

TIM SALMON

has a very easy swing—it's no effort for him to hit the ball 50 feet beyond the fence."

All-Star closer Troy Percival, meanwhile, churned out save after save in the late '90s. He broke the 30-save mark four times, hitting a high of 42 in 1998. Percival hardly ever changed speed. He preferred to challenge hitters straight-up, rearing back and firing an overpowering fastball that approached speeds of 100 miles per hour.

In **2000**, Mo Vaughn became the first Angels player in 13 years with two straight 100-RBI seasons.

As the Angels began play in the 21st century, they also relied on 275-pound first baseman Mo Vaughn, a former AL MVP. During his first two seasons with the Angels (1999 and 2000), the intimidating slugger hit a total of 69 homers. Unfortunately, after the Angels missed the playoffs for the 15th straight season in 2001, Vaughn was traded away to the New York Mets. Still, Anaheim fans

MO VAUGHN

Third baseman
Troy Glaus
was known
for his
big bat
and strong
throwing arm.

TROY GLAUS

Dominant closer Troy Percival struck out 71 batters in 57 innings of work in **2001**.

TROY PERCIVAL

were confident that such players as newly acquired pitcher Aaron

Sele would help carry the Angels back to the postseason in the

The Angels
counted on
the continued
fine play of
Ben Molina,
an excellent
defensive
catcher.
years ahead.

The Angels have been part of southern California's

fun and sun scene for parts of five decades. Although

the team has won three division titles over those

years, it has yet to experience the thrill of a World

Series. Now, after a number of near-misses, the Angels appear ready

to soar into contention once more.

BEN MOLINA